Chakras

How To Open Your Chakras And Third Eye For
Happiness And Health

*(Let Your Aura Glow And Energy Flow While You
Cleanse Your Chakras)*

Brendon Andersen

TABLE OF CONTENT

Chakras: What Are They And How Do They Affect You? 1

Relations And Chakras 20

What Are Chakras? 51

Chakra Meditation 56

The Solar Plexus Chakra: Jupiter's Residence 65

A Wholesome Solar Plexus Chakra 70

Mudras And Pranayama: Their Effectiveness 80

Interpreting Auras 103

Throat Chakra 123

Chakra Stones 142

Chakras: What Are They And How Do They Affect You?

Do you feel that you have a hard time talking to other people? Do you ever feel as if your thoughts are jumbled? Do you often struggle with feelings of shame and rage? You could be dealing with a chakra imbalance or something else if you are experiencing any of these problems in your life.

Our energy centers, known as chakras, are situated directly along the body's midline. There are seven main ones, while some schools of chakra theory also mention a few other ones. Your body will feel amazing, you will be able to be genuine to yourself and to others, and you will be able to express the appropriate amount of love when all of these chakras are functioning properly and getting the energy they need. Your life will essentially be balanced if you don't suffer from any of the typical maladies that most people complain about.

On the other side, if something isn't going the way you want it to, you need to spend some time working on your chakras. Your chakras are not functioning properly if you have frequent fits of rage and jealousy, experience physical discomfort, have trouble focusing, or experience any of the other symptoms listed above.

These chakras may cooperate as well. If you discover that one is malfunctioning or not opening as it should, and you don't correct it straight away, ultimately the other chakras will also go out of alignment. The chakra or chakras that are irritating you need to be your main attention before the rest of them may begin to align themselves correctly.

There will be varying degrees of activity in each chakra. The chakras are said to be functioning normally when they are wide open and letting the energy pass through.

All of the chakras should ideally contribute to who we are. All of us have instincts, and when they are functioning correctly, they may have an impact on how we think and feel. This is not typically the case, however, since our intuition and the chakras will not be functioning correctly. It's possible that certain chakras aren't fully opened. All the chakras will become hyperactive when one or two of them are weak, which may lead to a variety of problems.

All of the chakras will function harmoniously and in harmony in the optimum condition. It will be more difficult to live a life where the chakras are functioning properly as a result of our contemporary lifestyles. We hardly have time to take care of ourselves since we are always rushing about trying to get everything done. But you must take a step back and understand how to take care of these chakras if you want to really experience a nice life that is joyful and healthy.

Fortunately, there are a number of strategies you may employ to balance the chakras after you identify which one is out of balance and needs to be corrected. The strategies will mostly assist you in opening up the necessary chakras since doing so will often resolve concerns with the other chakras being always hyperactive.

An overview of the chakras' history

The chakras are a part of a long-forgotten tradition, but they are beginning to surface once again. There are several fresh interpretations of their significance and how they work, and since there are so many different ways to conceptualize these chakras, it may often be simple to get confused. Although the chakras are becoming more well-known due to their growing popularity, there are still many instances when the information is incorrect, contradictory, or even incomprehensible. Before attempting to include the chakras into your life, it is vital to comprehend some of the history associated with them so that you may better grasp how to employ them.

The Vedas are among the earliest written traditions from India, having been preserved from the Brahmins of the upper caste's oral legacy. The term "chakra" originally meant "wheel" and was used to describe the chariot wheels that the monarchs of that era utilized. The term has also been employed in ancient books as a metaphor for the sun, which may travel the globe like a victorious chariot and will signify the endless wheel of time, which also symbolizes balance and order and is what the chakras will emphasize.

A new period was claimed to have begun with the chakras' birth, and they were often depicted as being preceded by a disk of light, similar to the halo of Christ, but there was also a spinning disk in front of them. The deity Vishnu is also claimed to have come to Earth with the charka, a club, a conch shell, and a lotus flower in his possession.

Many various versions of these literature, such as Patanjali's Yoga Sutras and the Yoga Upanishads, make reference to the chakras as being similar to psychic centers of awareness. The underlying purpose of yoga was to transcend nature and the environment in which one lives in order to realize a pure awareness that was free from any oscillations brought on by the emotions and the mind. The realization that occurs between awareness and realizations must eventually reintegrate with nature to get a better synthesis, yet the term "yoga" means "yoke" or "union."

It is thus no surprise that they are often connected with one another as the concepts of yoga and chakras emerged within the same lineage, the Tantric tradition. Because the chakras were both formed in the same traditions and may be utilized simultaneously, as we will explore later, you will discover that yoga is one of the ways that you will be able to align the chakras.

There are seven fundamental chakras according to conventional theories, and each one will reside within your body. Modern physiology makes it simple to observe that the seven chakras will perfectly match the body's primary nerve ganglia, all of which originate from the spinal column. Although many people believe that the chakras no longer affect them, they were strategically placed in areas of the body where there are nerves and where various regions might affect how the rest of the body would respond. It's intriguing that, even before all of the nerves and pressure points would have been recognized, the chakras were able to grow based on these ideas.

There are a few smaller chakras that are referenced in the ancient tasks in addition to the famous seven chakras, which are the ones on which most people focus. If you chose to go more into the ancient scriptures, you may uncover further alternatives as well. For instance, the soma chakra may be found just above the third eye chakra, and the Ananda Kanda lotus can be found next to the heart chakra.

Many individuals believe that the chakras are an outdated concept that you shouldn't bother with. They reason that the chakras have nothing to do with how they conduct their contemporary lives and may believe that it is all just made-up mysticism. However, in actuality, you will discover that the chakras are more significant now than they have ever been. We must be aware of how quickly we might lose our equilibrium. We constantly rush about, are anxious and stressed out, and often struggle in some of our personal relationships. The best way to bring things back into balance is using chakras.

When compared to others who don't even believe in the chakras and continue to experience all of the negative aspects of their life, those who practice chakra balancing are often lot healthier, happier, and better able to get through the day. Making sure that you may live the fantastic life you want free from problems is absolutely worth your attention.

The advantages of chakra balancing

The chakras must be balanced if you want to be in the greatest possible health, despite your belief that this is an old therapeutic technique that won't accomplish anything for you. You'll find it simpler to feel good and control your emotions as a result.

Chakra balance offers many advantages that are directly related to several of yoga's philosophical tenets. You will be able to comprehend the whole body integration that will occur after you have completed one of these sessions if you have practiced yoga before, either in a class setting or on your own. However, these two are closely connected and will enable you to be in the greatest health possible. We'll talk more about the advantages of incorporating yoga into your practice to balance the chakras later.

Numerous problems are said to be possible when the energy of a chakra, or more than one chakra, is blocked. It may cause you to have severe sickness and agony in the obstructed location. You may feel distracted, struggle in your relationships, lose your creativity, experience pain, and a host of other negative effects. You will discover that it is simpler than ever to bring things back to normal and lessen some of the disease, pain, and other troubles that you are experiencing when you start to put the chakra theory into practice and focus on mending some of these problems using yoga and other techniques.

The many chakra types in the body

As was already said, there are about seven primary chakras visible within the body, and each is crucial to your general health and welfare. The seven are the most significant, however sometimes there are a few more that are included. The main chakras that will be covered in this article include:

The root chakra is all about physically being there and acquiring the ability to feel at home in a variety of circumstances. If this chakra is open, you will feel grounded, safe, and secure. You won't feel the need to be suspicious of those close to you, and you'll be able to spend more time living in the now than daydreaming. If you find that you experience anxiety and dread often, your root chakra is probably not functioning properly. If it is hyperactive, you could feel a little materialistic and greedy and are probably preoccupied with security, which makes you resistant to change.

The sacral chakra is all about your emotions and your sexuality. Your emotions will flow easily and be simple to convey when the sacral chakra is open, preventing you from becoming unduly emotional over it. You may feel alive and passionate, and there won't be any problems with your sexuality. You will be receptive to this connection. If you experience stiffness or lack of feeling, the sacral chakra may be a little underactive. On the other side, your sacral chakra is hyperactive if you always feel emotional or if you think you are emotionally tied to other people.

The nice thing about the navel chakra is that it is all about having the confidence to stand out for yourself in a group. You'll feel like you have control over your life and have a healthy degree of self-esteem when this chakra is open. When this chakra is underactive, you will feel frightened, unable to get the things you want, unsure of your course of action, and inactive. However, if your navel chakra is overactive, you'll probably come out as aggressive and tyrannical.

Heart chakra: the heart chakra is associated with love, compassion, and affection. When this chakra is open, you are more approachable and sympathetic, and you can ensure that all of your interpersonal interactions are as harmonious as possible. When your heart chakra is underactive, you'll show characteristics of being chilly and distant. You will, however, go in the other way if the chakra is hyperactive. People may likely feel as if you are practically smothering them with your affection, which often has some self-serving motivations.

The throat chakra is the one for speaking and expressing oneself. You will discover that there are less issues with self-expression when it is opened up just enough, and if that is how it works for you, you may even employ this expression as an artist. You may not speak out much and tend to be quiet and reserved when the throat chakra is underactive and not functioning as it should. Additionally, lying sometimes blocks this chakra. When this chakra is hyperactive, you will often talk excessively, generally dominating the discussion, and it might make others shy away from you. This may also be true if you have poor listening skills.

The chakra associated with visualization and insight is the third eye. When it's wide open, you'll probably spend a lot of time daydreaming and often exhibit strong intuition. If your third eye chakra isn't functioning correctly, you could find it difficult to think things through on your own and that you depend on other people to tell you what to do. Additionally, you are someone who is often confused. You can find yourself spending too much time in the realm of imagination if the third eye chakra is hyperactive.

The crown chakra is all about knowledge and discovering how to live in harmony with the rest of the planet. When this chakra is fully open, you will be well-aware of the outside world and free from bias toward both yourself and other people. You may not have a strong sense of your spirituality if the head chakra is not functioning properly. Additionally, you'll have a somewhat strict style of thinking. You'll likely overthink things if your head chakra is hyperactive. You can even start disregarding some of the physiological necessities that you should be focusing on because of your addiction to your spirituality.

As you can see, there are several kinds of chakras, and each one will benefit various sections of your body. You will be in touch with your spirituality, experiencing a lot of love for those around you, being very creative, able to think about all of the different things that you should do without overthinking things, and simply being at one with other people, yourself, and the world that is around you when they are working well together.

However, things will start to go out of balance and your thinking, your relationships, and even certain physical things won't function as they should when one or more of the chakras are out of alignment, blocked up, or open up excessively. It may be challenging to feel well as a result, and you may worry about how to get better. While the majority of us do not link these problems to our chakras, often focusing on one or two of these chakras can quickly produce results.

The chakras are a fantastic method to take care of your body and ensure that your body and mind will function effectively with one another, as well as with other people in your immediate environment and even with yourself. Finding the chakra type that is most problematic and then providing it the treatment it requires to open up and restore your health might take some time. We'll go through some of the alternatives you'll need, such as color therapy, practicing meditation, and even putting more yoga in your routine, to make sure you can realign your chakras and start feeling better right away.

Relations And Chakras

There are said to be seven main sorts of relationships that people experience throughout their lives. Each of the seven chakra centers—your sacral chakra, solar plexus, root chakra, crown chakra, heart center, throat chakra, and brow chakra—is represented by one of the seven relationship kinds that we have. The Vedas claim that the chakra that is strongest or most active during a relationship defines its purpose or objective.

The pair of the root chakra

The sexual energy that exists between couples rules the root chakra. This represents the chakra of the survival instinct since it reveals the couple's propensity for having children. This chakra rules over us and affects how we bear children and carry on our family tree. This also gives us the ability to defend ourselves and keep ourselves safe from harm. Therefore, this chakra is linked to selfishness. This chakra serves as our motivation, hence it is ego-driven. This permits us to advance our objectives and protect ourselves from being exposed. This pair wants to be intimate physically. Couples with root chakras often cross paths in public settings like bars, clubs, parties, and other social gatherings. The goal is often to locate a spouse or wife or other kind of long-term companion. This kind of marriage tends to have a particularly lengthy or intense honeymoon time since Mars is their governing planet.

They have frequent, intense love experiences, which eventually pass. Due to the initial powerful and passionate emotion, this fading away and drifting apart causes a little bitter attitude or disappointment. They often experience feelings of love as a result of the physical connection. Additionally, there is no particular balance in this kind of relationship. It features abrupt highs and lows rather than smooth transitions. In the relationship, there are often many opposing emotions, including love and hatred. These couples often hurry into marriage or postpone their nuptials for an undetermined amount of time. The marriage endures despite the relationship's propensity for instability because of the couple's emotional dependency rather than simply simple love.

The pair of sacral chakras

The sacral chakra is tuned to by the pair of the sacral chakra. This kind of chakra links the spiritual energy between partners and is linked to contentment, self-assurance, and ingenuity. Despite how pleasant these traits are, the chakra may also tend toward unfavorable feelings like avarice, fear, and self-preservation. This couple's dominant chakra often produces stability. The pair has a growing sense of love as a result of this sort of chakra. It results from a shared desire for peace, prosperity, and comfort. Venus is the planet that rules over chakras of this sort. This kind of chakra values spirituality or interpersonal peace. When two or more people with sacral chakra dominance meet together, they initially feel themselves at ease and in harmony with one another.

Their root chakra doesn't begin to take over until they are at ease with one another and feel at home together. This develops a deeper level of romanticism and a shared knowledge of one another. Because they cooperate rather than relying only on physical closeness and passionate romance, this results in a highly solid partnership. However, since this chakra is a lesser energy center, it causes more sadness and discontent than bliss. This kind of partnership has comfort as its primary goal. Couples decide to be a little materialistic in order to cope with this comfort, and this becomes their objective. These couples also fall under the category of the opulent. They have a number of automobiles, fancy residences, opulent interiors, and other things in an effort to make their neighbors envious. This kind of connection grows in snobby environments like pricey concerts, exclusive social events, costly restaurants, elaborate dinner parties, etc.

Couple from the solar plexus

The fundamental force of all of our energy chakras is formed by this kind of chakra. This particular chakra is linked to our aspirations and objectives. There are two main categories of ambition or goal-setting. The first category includes substantial materialistic pleasures like luxurious homes, expensive automobiles, trips, etc. This kind is connected to the sacral chakra as well. Prestige, power pride, and adulation are examples of the opposite sort of ambition. Couples with this sort of dominant chakra seek each other out for their reputation and power. The marriages of famous people are an excellent illustration of the Solar Plexus pair. The sun is this sort of chakra's most prominent characteristic and the house it rules, therefore it stands to reason that this type of coupling would have influence. This particular chakra type encourages individuals to establish themselves and find a position in society. In this kind of relationship, it is challenging to establish harmony and tranquility. This is a result of the high standards that couples set for one another during the relationship. They would need to lessen their expectations of one another if they were to get along and build a solid partnership based on shared affection. Additionally, this kind of partnership has a selfish and domineering tendency. It takes selflessness and submission for this kind of partnership to function.

Couples of this kind are driven, focused, and set high standards for themselves. Conflicts arise only after they have achieved the intended result. Everybody begins to develop an ego, which causes conflicts and resentments. These kinds of couples often cross paths at social gatherings, exclusive occasions, sporting events, political propaganda, and so on. These couples are good goal-setters with strong self-esteem and objectives that motivate them to maximize their potential. They often succeed from a young age and have a tendency to be haughty. They have great managerial abilities. They are able to persuade others to adopt their point of view because they are natural leaders. With more honors to their credit, they also grow smug. Couples of this kind often don't meddle in one another's personal lives because of this.

They concentrate on realizing their full potential and elevating their own reputation and esteem in society. People also have a tendency to hunt for partners who can help them become more well-known and prestigious in this environment, and when this doesn't happen, they try to alter their spouses for them, which may be frustrating. The pair gradually feels cut off from one another as a result of this, and they grow distant from one another. This causes disillusionment, and eventually, these couples only stay together for the sake of reputation and mutual profit.

the romantic pair

Since the Heart Centered Couple is associated with one of the high-level energy centers, their relationships are often fruitful and stable. This suggests that the pair may have long-term fulfillment and contentment, resulting in long-lasting relationships. This group of couples strives to grow as individuals and as a couple. They are driven to pursue happiness and pleasurable activities. Including making other people happy. They actively engage in charitable giving, volunteer work, and community involvement. They avoid impediments and strive to make the other person happy.

They often have a good understanding of their spouses, which makes their relationships generally last. Their friendship allows them to expand their social circle and meet new pals. They maintain principles that bind them together and have excellent morals. Their goal is to achieve tranquility and comfort. These folks often have a positive outlook and follow their hearts. They are full of goodwill and wish others well. They have a strong feeling of obligation and drive to give back to society. They are kind, sincere, and trustworthy. They allowed the romance to develop without them. They spend time getting to know one other and taking the effort to comprehend relationships. They are harmonious couples because the moon has an effect on them. Additionally, they really care about their spouses.

They often do not encounter obstacles or issues that may make it difficult for them to survive. They often work together to overcome these challenges without harming one another, which inevitably deepens their love and respect for one another. Typically, they strive to improve themselves and shape themselves into their ideal selves. Additionally, they do not have a particularly high view of spirituality.

the pair of throat chakras

Sharp perceptions are common among those who fall under the throat chakra. Additionally, they strive to master these senses and engage in activities that might heighten them. They often meditate in an effort to uncover the mysteries of the cosmos. They are sincere and wish everyone great pleasure. They are ruled by the planet Mercury. They are often non-materialistic in character and possess qualities like honesty and self-control. They are not egoistic and have a stronger propensity towards spiritual pursuits. They do not make rash decisions or act on emotional whims. They give things some consideration and take some time to do so. Through their great senses, they attempt to connect with the cosmos. They also don't pay attention to worthless stuff like drama, unrequited dialogues, or gossip. Additionally, they lack arrogance and conceit. They don't act haughtily or look down on other people. They are plain and modest. They often follow their own advice. Due to this, it is rather difficult to find these couples. They possess a strong sense of intuition and purpose. They are elegant in their actions and maintain peaceful silences. They have a keen sense of aesthetics and detail. Their sophisticated and exceptional taste in music, art, and literature demonstrate this. They connect to one another and have empathy for one another. They have great communication skills and are drawn to one another by vibrations. They are in happy marriages, and it is because of them that the idea of a soul mate is born. Additionally, they are tuned into one another and thoroughly comprehend what their spouse is thinking and wanting. They collaborate over distances as well, and their keen intuition makes it simple for them to select a matched companion. Simply by observing another individual, one could know that they are that other's mate.

Couple of the third eye chakra

Relationships of this kind are the result of self-actualization or self-realization. Couples in this chakra are governed by the planet Saturn. They often connect spiritually and psychically with one another. They engage in basic, calm activities like meditation. They are devoted to one another and give each other their life. They spend their whole lives thinking and reflecting. They are dedicated to discovering the utmost truth and comprehending the universe, and they have a healthy perspective on things. Spiritual leaders and instructors encounter this kind of interaction via a spiritual framework. They have an extremely unselfish mentality since they don't exist for themselves but for others. They strive to maintain harmony amongst their couples. They may or may not refrain from having sexual contact with one another, but they place more of an emphasis on their relationship's introspective components.

The pair of the crown chakra

Romantic relationships are those that come under the head chakra. They had the kind of love and passion seen in fairy tales. They belong to Jupiter's solar system. While they are amorous, they often avoid touching and being intimate with one another. These kinds of partnerships often see their spouses as mentors. The spouse adopts a saintly way of living, emphasizing the spiritual rather than the interpersonal components of the relationship. The wife's gaze on her spouse is similar to a teacher's. They are devoted to one another and have a teacher-disciple relationship with one another.

The chakra system and its effects

Although the sacral chakra is the book's main emphasis, this is a very brief and straightforward overview of the seven other chakras.

First Chakra: Root

Stability, adrenal function, survival, ego, practicality, assurance, and energy allocation are all factors in reproduction. In addition to red, the root chakra also has the colors black and dark brown.

In this color spectrum, healing gems like ruby, red garnet, hematite, black onyx, and red jasper may be used.

Second chakra: Sacral

Sexuality, fertility, reproduction, intuition, emotions, and creativity are all genito-urinary-related.

1" lower than the navel. together with the genitalia.

Sexuality, emotion, desire, creativity, intuition, and self-worth are all balanced in this. If it's obstructed, you could experience emotional instability, low energy, and feelings of loneliness. Physically, it may cause lower back pain, impotence, prostate issues, renal and uterine difficulties, and impotence.

The sacral chakra is orange in color.

Carnelian, orange calcite, aragonite, amber, and orange sapphire are crystals.

Third Chakra: Solar Plexus

digestive: emotions, stress, the pancreas, the stomach, and self-confidence.

situated behind the stomach and behind the breastbone. It is located directly below the shoulder blades as seen from the back of the body.

It is sometimes referred to as the "power chakra" and is linked to the brain, the central nervous system, aspiration, fury, and joy. You may lack confidence, worry about other people's views, be too sensitive to criticism, have poor self-esteem, or have an addictive nature if this chakra is blocked.

Physically, it may address conditions including allergies, diabetes, chronic tiredness, and stomach ulcers.

Citrine, yellow sapphire, topaz, golden tiger's eye, yellow jasper, and yellow sapphire

Chakra 4: Heart

Circulatory: immune system, love, compassion, healing, and personal development.

located in the heart region, at the center of the chest.

It is linked to spirituality, love, and compassion. When this chakra is out of balance, you may experience feelings of indecision, paranoia, fear of betrayal, or overall self-pity. On a physical level, it may cause malignancies, high blood pressure, lung illness, asthma, and heart disease. It may also apply to issues with the fingers, hands, and arms.

Colors: pink and green

Aventurine, malachite, jade, peridot, and emerald crystals are all green.

Pink: unakite, rose quartz, morganite, kunzite, and rhodochrosite

Fifth chakra: throat

Hearing, the lymphatic system, the respiratory system, and the creative and expressive processes

Located in the neck's throat region, right below the collar bone.

It is linked to speaking and writing as creative outlets for self-expression, voice, and communication. You may sense the want to hold back, the difficulty to express your emotions, inhibited creativity, or perfectionism if the energy is out of balance. Physically, it may treat tinnitus, hearing and thyroid issues, colds, sore throats, and other ailments.

Lapis lazuli, sodalite, aquamarine, sapphire, blue lace agate, turquoise, chrysocolla, and turquoise are some examples of crystals.

sixth chakra: third eye

Pituitary, eyes, mental and emotional stability, comprehension, and mental organization comprise the autonomic nervous system.

located directly above and between the eyes.

It is linked to psychic abilities, spiritual energy, and the eradication of egocentric mindsets. If it's out of whack, you could feel conceited or fearful of success, depending on the situation. Physically, it may result in migraines, night terrors, visual issues, eye difficulties, or neurological disorders.

Amethyst, sugilite, charoite, fluorite, lepidolite, and iolite are some crystals.

7th chakra: the crown
Mental acuity, awareness, perception, nerves, sleep, intuition, and inspiration are all functions of the central nervous system. positioned slightly above the top of the head at the crown.

This chakra is linked to knowledge, vitality, enlightenment, and spirituality. There may be an ongoing sensation of annoyance, bewilderment, despair, preoccupation, or lack of pleasure if this chakra is blocked. Physically, it may encompass epilepsy, chronic fatigue, or a susceptibility to toxins.

Crystals include tanzanite, selenite, danburite, amethyst, and pure quartz.

Chakra Healing Techniques

To maintain the balance of your Chakras and promote self-healing, you may combine a variety of techniques. For each chakra, they are divided into the following categories:

Simple Methods
Yoga Pose
Crystals
Mudras
Aromatic oils
Affirmations

Here is some helpful information for some of these activities, like crystals, mundras, essential oils, and affirmations, before we go into each of these techniques for each chakra. Yoga positions are really simple. You may begin your practice with 20 minutes and then extend it as necessary. The positions don't all have to be done at once, but you should concentrate on one chakra at a time.

Instruction Manual for Crystals

The techniques listed below are not the only ways to employ crystals for chakra healing, I should note before moving on. These are only ideas to get you going. As you go, you'll learn which one suits your needs the best and develop a special technique for chakra healing with stones.

You may utilize any crystal for any chakra, even if there are particular stones and hues for certain chakras. If necessary, you may help balance by using a mix of stones for that chakra.

Following are some crystal cleansing and chakra balancing instructions:

Crystal Cleansing of All Major Chakras

Locate a serene area. Diffuse essential oils to create a calming atmosphere.
Lean back and lie down.
To facilitate the flow of energy, place the crystals in the designated chakra

placements, beginning with the Root Chakra.

Concentrate first on your Root Chakra. Think about the chakra, its color, how it spins, and the advantages of balancing it. Advance toward the Crown Chakra.

Keep the crystals in place while you're resting still for 15 to 30 minutes.

Remove each crystal one at a time, beginning with the one closest to your Crown Chakra, after you are entirely at ease.

Cleaning a certain chakra or chakras

You may choose to conduct any or all of the following to cleanse a specific chakra:

Use the crystal for the associated chakra as a meditation tool. Say your intentions while holding the crystal.

Wear gems that match the chakra that is out of harmony.

Put seven healing crystals related to the seven chakras in a portable bag that you can take with you.

Put your crystals next to your bed.

How to Use Mudras: A Guide

Every therapeutic method has certain guidelines. Keep the following in mind while applying mudras to cure chakras:

Do's

On an empty stomach, practice mudras in the morning and the evening. Mudra practice requires at least a four-hour interval after a meal.

A mudra should be held for at least 15 minutes and as long as 45 minutes every day. If you have a limited amount of time, you might divide the session into two and practice while your stomach is empty. For the best results, it is strongly advised to commit to the same time each day.

Sitting in a meditation stance like Lotus stance or Thunderbolt Pose, practice mudras.

If you practice yoga, do mudras after you've finished your practice of breathing exercises.

Don'ts

If you don't need to use mudras to address painful or heavy bleeding during your period, avoid doing them when you're on your period.
During the first seven months of pregnancy, avoid using mudras. If a problem has to be resolved, you must do the mudra while being guided by an expert.
While using mudras, do not ignore the need to urinate.

Instruction Manual for Essential Oils

Here are some tips on how to utilize essential oils for the best outcomes.

For topical treatment, diluted the essential oil with a carrier oil. The best suggestions would be to use castor oil, olive oil, jojoba oil, or coconut oil. On the area of the chakra that needs to be healed, you may apply the oil. You may gently massage the oil on your feet to repair the Root Chakra.

Use aromatherapy with essential oils. Diffuse the necessary essential oil while you are unwinding, doing meditation, or concentrating on chakra healing.

Three drops of essential oil are added to two liters of boiling water. breathe in the steam.

Take a soothing bath by adding a cup of baking soda and around 10 drops of essential oil to your bathtub.

Tips for using essential oils safely

Keep your youngsters away from your essential oils.

Before making a purchase, check the essential oil's shelf life.

Before usage, check for any possible negative effects.

Never store your essential oils in plastic. Glass bottles are the best option.

Use diluted essential oils whenever possible.

Only diffuse in well-ventilated places.

Women who are pregnant or nursing shouldn't use essential oil steam inhalation. It is very advised that a lady seek expert advice before utilizing essential oils at this time in her life.

Children should not be exposed to essential oils unless trained professionals are present. The dilution must be substantially more than it is for grownups typically.

Applying essential oils close to your lips, inner ears, or eyes is not advised.

A Guide for Making Affirmations

It's possible for affirmations to have a greater impact than one may think. However, adhering to the simple guidelines listed below can help your affirmations work:

Make strong affirmations that say you already have everything you need. If you're attending a job interview, you should say "I accept the job offer" rather than "I want the job." The phrase "Thanks for the job" is preferred over "I will get the job."

Make affirmations you can really believe in. Even if affirmations have the power to work like magic, making an affirmation that seems too ridiculous to you won't help you advance. If your affirmation is to give thanks to the world for providing you with a job that pays $10,000 per month and you make $1,000 per month, your mind may not make it happen since it won't be inclined to believe it. A 500- to 1,000-dollar increase affirmation you write will work wonders.

Keep your affirmations straightforward and sincere.

If you haven't achieved your aims significantly, occasionally evaluate your affirmations.

The secret to writing effective affirmations is acceptance. Create an affirmation that acknowledges the obstacle with a declaration that you are conquering it and going ahead to attain your goal if you have a certain characteristic or problem that prevents you from reaching it.

Trust your inner voice above all else; it will help you create the best affirmations to direct your success.

Let's examine these exercises for each chakra now.

Base Chakra

Maintaining the energy flow throughout your body by healing your root chakra. The Root Chakra maintains your sense of security and grounding.

There are many advantages to the yoga postures, crystals, mudras, and essential oils indicated here; we have chosen to focus on the advantages related to Root Chakra imbalances.

Simple Methods for Root Chakra Healing

Make use of red. With your eyes closed, see the Root Chakra as a bright crimson hue. Wear red as much as you can, including clothing and accessories.

Select a serene location and take a seat. Close your eyes and think about anything that causes an imbalance in your Root Chakra. Feeling uneasy is a fairly typical inclination for those with a weak Root Chakra. Believe that you can achieve security no matter what makes you uneasy. Take stock of all your blessings, including a fantastic family, amazing friends, and a tranquil job. Appreciate the resources you possess. You'll quickly experience ease and security.

Spend some time in your garden working and strolling. You will come into touch with earth, the Root Chakra's element.

No room at home for a garden? Not to worry. Take a stroll around a local park. Your sense of grounding will increase the more time you spend in nature.

Communicate better with others around you. You feel safe and confident when you strengthen your interpersonal interactions.

Dance. When you dance, you put your insecurities aside and concentrate on the steps. By doing so, you will become more conscious, which is crucial for balancing the Root Chakra. Additionally, dancing encourages you to let go of inhibitions and move freely. Your negativity vanishes, and your self-confidence soars.

Regularly practice yoga postures.

Have a pedicure; you're going to enjoy it. Your Root Chakra will function better the more you take care of your feet since taking good care of your feet will keep you grounded.

Use aromatic compounds.

For root chakra healing, use crystals.

Use the affirmations for the root chakra.

What Are Chakras?

It's crucial to comprehend what the chakras are and where they originate from before using them for healing and other energy activities. You will be better able to comprehend why chakras are significant and how they might benefit you when you are able to comprehend their history, place of origin, and precise nature. You will learn more about the chakras throughout the remainder of this book if you lay this foundational information around them.

Origins and History

The earliest Indian scripture, the Vedas, had information about the chakras between 1500 and 500 BC. Other scriptures and historical accounts, such as the Chudamini Upanishad, the Shri Jabala Darshana Upanishad, the Shandilya Upanishad, and the Yoga-Shikka Upanishad, have also made mention to these chakras, which are then written "cakra". The Ino-European people received oral tradition-based understanding of the complex chakra system. They were also known as Aryans. The chakra system was historically a component of Eastern philosophy; nevertheless, New Age writers found great resonance with the concept and made it more approachable for contemporary people via their work.

How Do Chakras Work?

In terms of its fundamental definition, a chakra is a rotating wheel or disk. A chakra is essentially thought of as a spinning disk on the body that channels energy. The chakras are energy centers that extend the whole length of your spine, from the "root" chakra at the base of the spine to the "crown" chakra at the top of your head. Although some more complex and in-depth writings claim that there are as many as 114 across the whole body and energy field, there are seven major chakras that span the length of your body.

The seven chakras that span the length of your spine are the main ones that are emphasized in spirituality, energy work, and healing. These chakras have a direct impact on a person's physical, mental, and emotional well-being. As a result, numerous techniques like energy healing and yoga closely align with the chakras to powerfully promote a state of wellness for everyone who chooses to partake in them.

Why Are There Chakras?

Expanding on the notion that chakras are spinning lights of energy over major body regions, you might come to understand that each one has a specific function directly related to the health of the body. They basically control how we perceive life psychologically when we are exposed to mental and emotional inputs. Every rotating disc adds to our total wellness, and we can immediately feel what our chakra is feeling, whether it's open or closed, balanced or out of balance, active or inactive, etc. You will notice a significant improvement in your general physical, emotional, and mental well-being when you work with these chakras to get them flowing smoothly.

Working with the chakras has a strong capacity to heal your energy, physical, and spiritual selves since they have the potential to significantly modify your state of being. You offer yourself the capacity to flow effortlessly through a healthy, enlightened, and balanced life when you remove any blockages from the chakra and balance them so that they operate in healthy flow. Our daily lives' physical, mental, and emotional equilibrium intimately linked to the harmony of our chakras. Working with them may help you get rid of a lot of unwelcome conditions you could have.

What More Should I Learn About Chakras?

Each chakra has a specific function and is situated in a separate location along your spine. They also have an impact on many organs and are related to certain diseases. Each has a distinctive hue. Additionally, they are intimately related to their own range of sensations, emotions, and actions. Once you identify which one is out of balance or out of alignment, you may focus on that one to treat the symptoms that are directly related to it.

The chakras are a highly developed energy body map that also directly affects our physical, mental, and emotional bodies. They appeared for the first time in writing between 1500 and 500 BC in some of the earliest writings ever discovered. Chakras are a potent chance for you to discover how to balance your body and treat a wide range of illnesses for which you may struggle or suffer. You'll probably discover that doing so greatly benefits your overall wellness.

Chakra Meditation

Perhaps you see reflection as an example of someone crossing their legs and muttering to themselves. Contemplation is about more than just this, however. There are many different sorts of contemplation that might help you relax and relieve stress. Chakra is a specific kind of contemplation that is based on Hindu principles. The art of chakra reflection is being practiced all across the world.

Chakra meditation is a sort of contemplation that includes several relaxing techniques targeted at bringing balance, tranquility, and prosperity to the chakras. An archaic Sanskrit term with Indian roots, "chakra" conjures up images of a wheel or vortex.

Chakras are the seven main centers of vital energy that govern each of our individual bodily parts as well as various elements of the mind in the human body.

Along a section of the human spinal column, they are located next to a hormonal organ.

Chakras may get blocked, and if even one of the seven chakras does, it can lead to bodily or emotionally charged conflicts, neither of which are necessary.

Chakra Meditation Techniques: How Do They Work?

The earth and the organs located throughout our bodies and the circulatory system get the incredible life-force energy that is circulated throughout our amazing and perplexing cosmos. The secret to achieving optimal prosperity and wellness is this life-power vitality. It is believed that since the chakras are connected, they actively work to equalize each other to the best of their ability.

Make every cell in your body tremble and rejoice!

Many of us have energetic squares and uncomfortable personalities together with vitality-attacking tendencies that prevent us from reaching our full essentialness, which makes us feel exhausted, scattered, dull, and sometimes even ill.

The Advantages of Meditating

If one is new to meditation, concerns about one's ability to practice it may arise, raising queries like "How would I consider nothing?" or "I can't do that." It can appear to be odd to attempt to discharge ourselves from the pending negative issues in life by what may appear to be a straightforward demonstration of sitting idle, particularly when compelling, passionate battles can mist our psyche.

When the weight of the outer world is weighing you down so heavily, it may be difficult to clear your brain, yet doing so becomes more important during these difficult times in daily life. I was overtaken by a different way of looking at life when I started to ruminate. These are only a couple of proposals from an energetic tenderfoot that may enable somebody to start a remunerating routine with regards to reflection and mindfulness.

Checking during respiration is a practice that has assisted me in keeping my mind in the optimal state for reflection. As I breathe in, I count until I've completed inhaling, which is typically around eight for me but can be anything depending on how quickly or slowly you count. As I exhale, I arrive at the same number, eight by the time I've completed my exhalation. Reiterating this procedure, I count to eight while inhaling through my nostril and then count to eight while exhaling through my mouth.

Cool air in, some circulation into heated air. I have also found it beneficial to visualize my inhalation as cold, positive energy entering my lungs and warm, negative energy that has been accumulated inside being expelled. Every breath is imagined, with the positive, fresh cloud entering through the nostril and the negative, stagnant cloud being expelled through the mouth.

Focus on a particular object. Focusing on a particular article is an additional technique that can be utilized to promote reflection. The object could be anything. Typically, I imagine a single light illuminated in a dark environment with no other objects nearby. I observe it glimmer while thoughts pass through my mind, aware of them but giving them no thought. According to my understanding, this type of meditation has been utilized to aid in the recovery of specific body parts.

Utilize sound while deliberating. A bit excessive, but something that has helped me a great deal, playing a sound can aid in "timing" sessions, freeing me from considering how much I've been considering. Occasionally, the application of sound can expedite the attainment of greater profundity.

However, I live in a home with five children, so putting on earplugs and covering up for twenty minutes is sometimes the best way for me to concentrate on thinking.

Daily practice is essential. The more you accomplish something, the easier and straightforward it becomes. This holds true for contemplation as well. It cultivates a healthy propensity for taking a pause and appreciating the present, traits that are all too often neglected in our hectic modern lives. The more you practice, the more doors will open up for you.

I'm still relatively new to the practice of contemplation, so I understand the concern with freshness. However, I cannot disregard the benefits of reflection as I read about them and experience them for myself, which further supports the notion that we are responsible for our own condition. Moreover, as I continue with my contemplation routine, I am pleasantly surprised by the positive vitality I experience when making the effort to find myself.

Health Advantages of Energy Healing

It is interesting to note that according to a November 2012 American Heart Association study on the impact of pressure reduction programs utilizing reflection, contemplation significantly reduces the risk of stroke, cardiovascular failure, death, anger levels, and coronary supply route disease.

Members of the program who meditated twice a day for a total of 20 minutes each day have experienced significant benefits. They had the option to reduce cardiovascular event and stroke risk by 48 percent. Furthermore, they reduced their levels of irritation. It is enthralling to note that the positive health benefits for members increase with the frequency of meditation sessions.

Adapting to continuous indignation is extremely harmful to the brain and body. There are certain things that one should give up or abandon if they have no wish for change. Not only are poisonous connections fatal, but they also impede recovery.

Chakra Music for Meditation and Chakra Colors to Meditate

In addition to other controls, music is also used to adjust the chakras. In addition to the music, the leader has included a number of amazing and dazzling images. These chakra vitality pigments are also an essential component of healing.

A sample of chakra colors includes green, which corresponds to the substance and emits extremely subdued damage. Indigo is a potent shade for the third eye that encourages us to see perfection regardless. Blue is also associated with the larynx chakra and the declaration of truth through speech.

Diverse techniques used to facilitate reflection include guided symbolism, body relaxation, perception, and breathing techniques. Whether you are aware of it or not, your Chakras are constantly operating within your body. They affect both your psychological and physical states. By lending special attention to these areas, you can influence them to enhance certain aspects of your existence.

The Solar Plexus Chakra: Jupiter's Residence

As a planet gains mass during its formation, nuclear processes are accelerated and a Sun is born. The greater a planet's mass, the brighter it becomes, and the greater the planet's brightness, the more heat it generates. Through this procedure, Jupiter approached the status of a second Sun!

Because of this, the ancient Romans referred to Jupiter as "the King of the Gods." Jupiter represents the archetype of the beneficent monarch, the opposite of Saturn's representation of the austere or dominant king. The concept of the "second Sun" provides insight into Jupiter's vitality; unlike the Sun, Jupiter does not bear the burdensome responsibility of fostering and nurturing all life. He is instead the bearer of good tidings, glad fortune, abundant plenty, and joyous celebration. He embodies the spiritual illumination that makes life worthwhile, the animating force of spiritual faith, religion, and higher learning, and the animating force of the entire universe, which is benevolence.

Jupiter is the psychological force that manifests as our propensity for altruism, selflessness, enthusiasm, optimism, and merriment. The energy of Jupiter is expansive, generous, exuberant, adventurous, and upbeat. Jupiter represents, above all, the psychological function that regulates and sustains faith in the inherent fairness of life.

Jupiter reveals the source of our vitality by revealing the essence of our capacity for happiness. There are activities, people, environments, and lifestyle choices that elevate our spirits and fundamentally reconcile us with the divine light that resides within each of us. Jupiter directs our attention to this inexhaustible and ever-flowing source of vitality and reveals the types of experiences and activities that inspire confidence in ourselves and in life.

Jupiter's glyph combines a perceptive crescent moon with the material actuality of a cross. This combination represents our capacity to perceive the potential of the material realm, while leading us to contemplate our capacity to expand physical and spiritual sustenance.

The sparkles of pleasure, joy, curiosity, and enthusiasm that propel us toward a job, a home, a relationship, or an activity are the flickering flames of Jupiter dancing within us. They are Jupiter's method of fostering the growth of vitality and self-assurance.

Constantly, the universe collaborates with us in our pursuit of happiness and alignment. The Universe wishes for us to be happy. Jupiter signifies the ways in which we can "play to our strengths" cosmically.

Therefore, on the one hand, the natal Jupiter indicates the types of activities or experiences that strengthen our faith in ourselves and strengthen our connection to a higher power or a positive outlook, and on the other hand, Jupiter indicates the manner or form in which our greatest opportunities and strokes of good fortune are most likely to manifest.

This archetype's shadow side is excessive confidence or optimism to the point of delusion. This Jupiterian quality is depicted on the 'Fool' Tarot card, which depicts a naïve adolescent carelessly stepping off the edge of a cliff with a casual expression. Jupiter's pathological aspect is exemplified by the sorrowful jester or tragic buffoon.

The constraints of common sense, prudence, and skepticism are abhorrent to Jupiter's vitality, and he abhors restrictions of any kind, especially rules. Jupiter desires to fly on the wings of his inspiration, and he is well aware that faith in oneself and one's beliefs have the power to move mountains.

However, faith alone is not always sufficient, and many Jupiterians suffer tremendously when their hubris, pomposity, and misguided schemes leave them bloodied and muddied in a ravine. At his unhealthiest, Jupiter can be nothing more than a glamorous shell inflated with illusions of valor and glory that no one else can see, and if he is so overconfident that he pursues a risky plan without the necessary support, a Jupiterian soul can suffer significant financial loss, injury, and humiliation.

Jupiter indicates where we are fortunate, but also where we must not take our good fortune for granted. It is difficult for Jupiter to retreat gracefully and even more difficult for him to admit defeat, not so much out of hubris as his innate optimism that "where there's a will, there's a way." Jupiter may experience a moment of resentment when he is denied the grandeur he believes is his birthright, but he is remarkably resilient. He is always resilient.

A Wholesome Solar Plexus Chakra

The Sacral Chakra Chakra is the core of our will, vitality, and strength. The third Chakra is governed by fire, which reflects the heat and tenderness of the dynamic energy that propels us forward.

Unlike the Root Chakra, which is naturally contracting and downward-flowing, the Third Chakra is expansive and perpetually ascending, like the embers of a fire. At the second Chakra, we became conscious of duality, which creates a fork in the road. At the third Chakra, we respond to these options by making decisions, or putting our will into action.

Will is the intentional control of change. Will is the transformative force of consciousness. The will Chakra is analogous to a portal through which the interior being not only interacts with the external world, but also actively modifies it in accordance with its conscious desires. Will is the union of thought and action.

We liberate ourselves from ingrained patterns and generate new behavior through our will. Our will prevents us from taking the path of least resistance and "playing it safe." It is the will that guides us when we want to break an addiction or free ourselves from ingrained patterns. To effect change, we cannot merely wait for favorable fortune to come to us; we must exercise our will.

The will consists of three components. First, there is excitement, the pleasant flare of interest, delight, or intrigue. To make anything meaningful occur, you must be invested with genuine, profound, engrossing inquiry and concern. This is the first item that actually gets you off the sofa and motivates you to take one particular path out of the many possible paths.

This spark of interest gives you the motivation to organize your life around your chosen priorities. Without enthusiasm or interest, life would be random disorder, with no energy directed toward the accomplishment of any particular goal.

The second characteristic of will is its vitality or power. You must infuse your idea with vitality. You must be able to marshal the available reserves of life force toward your consciously chosen objective. Our bodies' vitality is dependent on our ability to connect, integrate, and draw sustenance from our surroundings. We cannot create energy; we can only enable it to enter or prevent it from entering.

Likewise, we have no control over anyone or anything. We only have the ability to act. Attempting to compel or control others necessitates ceaseless focus and exertion, and ultimately depletes one's energy. True power derives from coordination and union in which each member possesses autonomy, free will, and personal agency. When each component contributes voluntarily from its own reserves of personal power, all in harmony and moving as one, we find the colossal forces that drive large-scale social movements, natural phenomena, awe-inspiring technological and architectural achievements, and collective shifts in consciousness. The origin of the greatest powers is unity and cooperation, not dominance. One of the most profound teachings of the Solar Plexus Chakra is the importance of striking an equilibrium between asserting oneself and allowing others to assert themselves.

The third characteristic of will is assurance or faith. Every endeavor entails a period of time during which you must maintain stamina, focus, effort, and concentration on your objective, well before it becomes manifest. You must believe it to be true. At this time, your trust and confidence are of the utmost importance. You must have a strong belief that you can accomplish your goals and that you truly merit what you desire.

The Solar Plexus controls our faith and trust, both in ourselves and in the beneficence of life itself. In any endeavor, our attitude is crucial and has a direct bearing on the outcome. The greater your confidence in the desired outcome, the more likely it is to materialize. People with an open Solar Plexus Chakra do not allow themselves to be dissuaded or discouraged by skeptics or doubters. They maintain an optimistic belief that they can accomplish anything they set their minds to, and it is this belief — even more than the effort expended in action — that determines whether their aspirations come true or not.

Exploration of the Sacral Chakra

Our body is 75% water, and the second chakra's element is water. This chakra is your delight, enjoyment, movement, and sensation center. The objective is to get things moving: to get your body moving, to move the vitality within, and to move your existence forward with pleasure. Pain causes us to contract, whereas pleasure causes us to expand.

Opening the second chakra to pleasure not only makes us feel joyful and more expansive, but it also moves subtle energy through the body, calming and releasing obstructions. Therefore, rather than "working" on this chakra, consider "playing!" Get outside and active! Dance, chant, vibrate, and allow yourself to experience the flow of your life force. Allow the rivers within you to flow into the ocean of ecstasy, and your energy will eventually migrate to the other chakras as well.

The second chakra is called Svadhisthana, which translates to "one's own sweet place."

In the same way that the first chakra is concerned with unity with the body, the second chakra allows us to enjoy the delights of duality. As we investigate our lives, we desire to experience various aspects of duality for enjoyment, such as the desire to rest and be passive and the desire for an intense activity that stimulates the mind and body.

The experience of polarity and the stimulation between the two extremes is what attracts our attention and stimulates the development of consciousness. As a result, we experience delight and the desire to pursue the next great opportunity in life.

Imagine receiving a massage; the body would open and unwind as it experiences delight. But if someone approached you and began to strike you, would your body not contract or refrain?

This is the result of experiencing discomfort rather than satisfaction. The chakras tend to close when they perceive a situation to be dangerous. This is especially true as we learn to discover our position in the world around the age of six months, when our developmental cycle begins. As the infant gains the ability to grasp and retain objects.

What is the child doing when it continues to collide into objects without comprehending what will cause injury or when it begins to place almost everything in its mouth? Using its five senses, the infant is discovering what causes delight and what causes suffering. It caresses everything, hears various noises, learns to taste... What happens if the infant enjoys the ice cream? He or she will want more! This is how he determines what delights are and how to avoid suffering as he ages.

But what if the child was repeatedly told not to do this or that, or that she or he is a naughty girl or boy, and made to feel humiliated over what we now consider to be trivial matters? Eventually, the infant ceases to articulate, which obstructs the second chakra.

The chakra remains deficient in energy because it has been retaining things within itself, not allowing the emotions to circulate, and not allowing the self to experience the pleasures of life in order to survive in the family and conduct as the mother or father (typically the primary caretaker) requests. Over time, they become emotionally apathetic and insensitive to their own feelings. Everything appears monotonous, and life begins to lose its significance and become mundane.

In my practice, I frequently observe individuals with overcompensatory responses to the obstruction of their second chakra. This leads to excessive expressions of emotion, such as excessive clinginess, fragile personal boundaries, or excessive expressions of emotion, sometimes including wrath and extremes of emotion.

This adult overexpression is rather a compensatory response to childhood inability to express and be validated. These individuals are incapable of relating to the emotions and sentiments of others and consider their comprehension to be absolute. They will continue to speak without regard for whether or not the other person is listening.

They are as oblivious of the emotions of those around them as they are of their own. As a result, they are oblivious of their own needs and desires and similarly incapable of comprehending and satisfying the needs and desires of those around them. Relationship pleasures fluctuate between extremes, and such individuals can become unpredictable to the point of becoming narcissistic.

A balanced chakra would mean being able to enjoy life's small pleasures, such as drinking tea with friends, reading a book, connecting with others on a deeper level, being able to empathize with others without being carried away - remaining detached from the sufferings of the outside world while still being able to relate to what's going on around them.

Utilize the following exercises to locate the location within yourself where you feel and experience profoundly.

Mudras And Pranayama: Their Effectiveness

Mudras and pranayama are potent instruments for opening and balancing the chakras in many spiritual traditions. Mudras are hand positions and gestures that leverage the energy of the mind, body, and spirit in order to align these energy centers. Pranayama is profound breathing that assists in activating and circulating the passage of vital life force (chi) throughout the body.

Regular practice of mudras and pranayama enhances our sense of well-being by facilitating the attainment of physical and energetic balance and harmony. Mudras and pranayama should be thoroughly investigated if you wish to access your inner power by energizing your chakras.

This chapter describes two useful additions that will enhance your meditation practice and help you to balance the sacral chakra. The mudras that assist to balance the energy of this chakra come first. The second is pranayama, a potent technique for enhancing energy transmission. In addition, it explains how to perform pranayama breathwork for chakra equilibrium to maximize your meditation experience.

Mudras

The body contains seven major chakras, or energy centers. Each chakra corresponds to a distinct color, element, and set of emotions. Chakra balancing promotes physical, mental, and emotional well-being. Hand gestures, or mudras, are a method for balancing the chakras.

Mudras may be utilized during meditation or when feeling out of balance. Each mudra corresponds to a distinct chakra. The Apana Mudra, for instance, is associated with the Root Chakra; it serves to ground and center you, thereby promoting stability and security. The Anahata Mudra is associated with the Heart Chakra; it assists in the opening and balancing of the heart chakra, thereby promoting love, compassion, and understanding.

Recommended for the sacral chakra is the Svadhisthana Mudra. This mudra enhances our capacity for enjoyment and creativity. A number of additional mudras are utilized to regulate the sacral chakra. Incorporating these mudras into your meditation practice will help you attain greater physical, emotional, and mental balance and harmony.

Experiment with various mudras to determine which ones are most effective. There is no correct or improper method. Simply follow your intuition and have faith that you will find the ideal mudra for balancing your chakras.

The Strength of Mudras

Mudras are essential instruments for balancing and healing the sacral chakra, or the emotional energy center. These ancient gestures have been used for thousands of years in yoga and meditation because they facilitate a connection to the divine energy that surrounds us. We direct this potent energy to travel through our bodies and restore balance to our sacral chakra by interlacing specific fingers or making specific finger movements.

Whether you use mudras prior to meditation or want to incorporate them into your daily life, their ability to access the sacral chakra makes them an immensely potent tool for attaining happiness, health, and tranquility. If you are searching for a means to leverage the power of your chakras, then you should investigate mudras.

Mudras for Opening the Sacral Chakra

You can use a variety of mudras to clear the sacral chakra and increase your energy flow. Among the most prevalent are the yoni mudra, the varun mudra, and the ksepana mudra. These mudras can assist you in balancing your sacral chakra and enhancing the movement of energy in your lower abdomen.

Which mudra you choose depends on your desired outcome. Yoni mudra is an excellent location to start if you're looking for a simple and straightforward method to clear the sacral chakra. Try the Varun mudra or the ksepana mudra to increase energy transmission within the body. Regardless of which mudra you choose, you should concentrate on your inhalation and visualize the area of your body you wish to access. With consistent practice, you should observe a difference in your energy levels and general sense of well-being.

Healing Sacral Chakra Mudras

There are numerous mudras for healing the sacral chakra. Among the most prevalent are the Prithvi mudra, the Apana mudra, and the yoni mudra. These mudras can assist in clearing the sacral chakra and enhancing the body's energy flow.

Prithvi mudra is utilized to enhance the body's earth element. This mudra can assist in balancing the energy in the lower abdomen, thereby enhancing physical and mental health. Apana mudra is a mudra used to increase water and earth energy in the sacral chakra. This mudra aids in resolving health issues associated with sacral chakra imbalances, such as urinary or reproductive issues.

The Various Mudras

When we activate and open our sacral chakra with mudras, we experience more pleasure in life by being present in the moment and appreciating all that it has to offer. There are numerous sacral chakra mudras, and each is associated with a distinct emotional quality. Among the most frequent mudras for balancing the sacral chakra are the following:

For each mudra we demonstrate, we will also clarify the significance of the appellation, the hand gesture, and their relationship to the sacral chakra.

Shakti Mudra - The Energy Gesture

The Sanskrit word "Shakti" translates to "power." Therefore, the Shakti Mudra is a mudra of fortitude and force. It assists in the activation of kundalini energy, or the vital force located at the base of the vertebrae. This mudra is frequently employed to enhance creativity, boost self-esteem, and regulate the sacral chakra. When we perform this mudra, we tap into our natural power and utilize it to accomplish our objectives.

Begin the Shakti Mudra by assuming a comfortable seated position with an upright spine. Place your hands on your knees with your palms facing upward and your index and middle fingers wrapped around your thumbs. Extend the ends of your little and ring fingers and connect them together. Now that the shakti mudra is complete, you may hold it for as long as you wish.

Slowly and thoroughly inhale and exhale while concentrating on the sacral chakra. Imagine a rotating orb of orange light in your lower abdomen. Imagine the orb of light expanding and becoming more brilliant as you exhale. Continue to focus on the sacral chakra and take long breaths until you sense your emotions balancing.

Yoni Mudra - The Universal Womb Position

Yoni mudra.

Yoni mudra is an ancient yogic practice thought to stimulate the sacral chakra, which is located in the lower genital region. This exercise entails creating a circle with the thumb and index finger and tracing a straight line from the navel to the solar plexus. Yoni mudra clears your sacral chakra of any obstructions or imbalances by connecting the energy from your body's base to its potential at your center.

When executing the yoni mudra: Straighten your back and place your hands in your lap with the palms facing up. Form a diamond by bringing the tips of your thumbs and forefingers together. Interlace your remaining fingers with the tips of your forefingers facing the earth. Visualize a red energy orb rotating in your sacrum, tap into it in your mind's eye, and continue to breathe while focusing intently on your sacral chakra.

If you're new to mudras, you should begin with the yoni mudra, which is one of the most common mudras for the sacral chakra. Whether you wish to enhance your creativity and intuition, initiate new romantic relationships, or release emotional trauma, this simple yet potent mudra can assist you. It allows you to access your inner knowledge and the potent energy of your sacral chakra.

Varun Mudra - The Water Gesture

Varun mudra is a gesture that represents the element of water. This mudra is frequently used to balance the sacral chakra and increase the body's energy flow. Its name derives from the Hindu deity Varuna, who is associated with water and the ocean. The Varun mudra invokes the creative and nurturing power of water, making it an ideal gesture for those who desire healing or inspiration.

Simply sit in a comfortable position with your back erect to perform the Varun mudra. Extend your hands in front of you with the palms facing upward. Touch the ends of your pinky and index fingers together, and then spread your other fingers. To balance the sacral chakra with the Varun mudra, focus your attention on the area between your navel and pubic bone. Imagine a rotating orb of blue light in this area. Imagine the orb of light expanding and brightening as you inhale and exhale. Continue to concentrate on your respiration and the water energy in your body until you experience the opening of your sacral chakra.

Varun mudra is an excellent starting point for balancing your sacral chakra if you need a fast and simple method. This mudra is basic and can be performed anywhere, making it an ideal choice for people with hectic schedules. Remember to take steady, deep breaths as you practice Varun mudra to maximize its benefits.

Ksepana Mudra - The Sealing Gesture

Ksepana mudra is a gesture that confines the sacral chakra's vitality. This mudra is commonly employed to remove energy obstructions from the body and increase energy flow in the lower abdomen. Additionally, it can balance the energy in other chakras, including the crown chakra and heart chakra.

To perform the ksepana mudra, sit with your hands on your knees and your spine erect. Connect the digits of each hand. Release the pointing fingers and fold the opposing thumbs over the opposite pointing finger. Now, force your knuckles just above your pubic bone into your lower abdomen.

As you breathe in and out, visualize a white light orb rotating in your lower abdomen. Concentrate on your respiration and the energy of the sacral chakra until you sense the opening of your lower abdomen. Ksepana mudra is a wonderful method to increase energy flow in the body and remove any blockages that prevent energy from flowing freely.

Pranayama

Breathing is not only a vital life function, but also a potent tool that can be used to promote physical and mental health. Pranayama is a yoga technique for calming the mind and body through controlled breathing. The practice is beneficial for focusing the mind during meditation, and it is also an effective method for relieving tension and promoting tranquility.

When the nervous system is in equilibrium, it is simpler to attain a state of calm and concentration. As one of the benefits of pranayama, controlled breathing assists in regulating the nervous system.

In addition, controlled respiration promotes better circulation and detoxification. Therefore, pranayama is an essential component of yoga practice and extremely advantageous for those who wish to enhance their overall health and well-being.

One of the most significant advantages of this practice is that it helps to open and balance the sacral chakra. Specifically, pranayama will aid in the discharge of any repressed emotions or stagnant energy. As a result, this practice is extremely advantageous for those who wish to expand their creativity or experience greater emotional liberation.

Pranayama helps regulate and direct the body's energy flow. By focusing on the breath and deepening inhalations and exhalations, we can move stagnant energy and open the passage of vital life force energy within the body. In addition to fostering creativity, pranayama strengthens the immune system, increases energy levels, and calms the mind.

The Various Forms of Pranayama

Pranayama is an essential component of any yoga practice, as it targets the various energy centers (or chakras) in the body and helps you attain improved physical, mental, and spiritual health. To activate the sacral chakra, some yogis use various pranayama techniques, such as alternate nostril breathing (Nadi shodhana), mula bandha, and abdominal rolls. These can be employed independently or in combination for a potent effect on the energy body. Regardless of your technique, pranayama helps you unlock and balance your sacral chakra for optimal health and vitality.

Here are some easy pranayama techniques to help you open and balance your sacral chakra:

Ujjayi Breath - Triumphant Breath

Ujjayi is a technique for respiration control that helps soothe the mind and promotes tranquility.

Implementing Ujjayi Breath

Take a long, deep breath through your nostril. While exhaling through the nostrils, make a "ha" sound. As you exhale, constrict the muscles at the back of your larynx to produce a faint wheezing sound. Repeat this for three to five minutes.

Alternating Nostril Breathing (Nadi Shodhana)

Nadi shodhana is a pranayama technique that purifies and cleanses the body's energy channels (or nadis). Typically performed prior to meditation to cleanse the mind and prepare for introspective concentration.

Performing nadi shodhana

Comfortably position your palms in a mudra (a hand position that helps direct the passage of energy). Close your right nostril with your right forefinger and inhale deeply through your left nostril. Release your right thumb and close your left nostril with the ring finger. Exhale through your right nostril, then inhale through the same nostril. Close your right nostril, release your left nostril, and exhale through your left nostril. Repeat this breath for three to five minutes, then alternate sides and repeat.

Mula Bandha - Root Lock

Mula bandha is a yogic technique that locks energy in the lower body and directs it to the higher chakras.

Performing Mula Bandha

As you inhale and exhale, simply contract the perineum (between your anus and genitals). This assists in directing the prana (vital energy) of the body toward the sacral and solar plexus chakras.

Stomach Rolls

Simple but effective pranayama technique for stimulating the sacral chakra are abdominal rolls.

Carrying out Belly Rolls

Simply take a long breath in and expand your stomach. Exhale and roll the pelvic forward while tucking the tailbone and curving the back. Repetition of this respiration for three to five minutes will help to open the pelvis and sacral chakra.

While these pranayama techniques are among the most fundamental in yoga, they have also been demonstrated to be highly effective for promoting sacral chakra balance. Use mudras (hand gestures) in addition to pranayama to open and balance your sacral chakra. Mudras are an essential component of yoga, as they help direct the movement of energy throughout the body and balance the various energy centers.

This chapter covered several of the most effective pranayama and mudra techniques for balancing and expanding the sacral chakra. Learn more about additional practices for the sacral chakra by reading the remainder of this book.

As the color associated with creativity, orange is a vivacious hue. This attractive combination of yellow and red contains a wealth of meaning and insight. This chapter will provide additional details.

The Color of Harvest

The sun is typically represented by orange or yellow. Orange represents the creative aspect of the sun that animates life on earth.

It is ironic that orange is the only fruit with the same designation as its hue. This is due to the fact that it is the hue of produce. In the autumn, when plants reach their peak before fading off for the winter, they frequently turn orange. Before it is carved into a frightening shape to signify death or Halloween, the pumpkin is a common symbol of this. Also, many leaves change orange prior to falling off and dying; this phenomenon is commonly referred to as the flowering of trees. Orange is also the color of flowers, although many are not literally orange. Similar to fruits, which contain seeds, flowers also cause reproduction (or serve a creative function). The inclusion of "sun" in the appellation of the "Sunflower" flower is not coincidental.

It is fascinating to note that what attracts has a creative function, similar to how humans who are attracted to one another marry to procreate. Fruit, foliage, and flowers allure us in various ways during harvest season so that they can propagate their seeds.

Surprisingly, the orange human chakra is also the location of the reproductive organs.

Orange: Color of the Sacral Chakra

The sacral chakra, also known as Swadhisthana in Sanskrit, is located in the pelvis region and is responsible for your emotions, feelings, relationships, expression, fantasies, and creativity.

As the center of your sensations and emotions, this chakra is related to the various sentiments you experience and express. This is why its color is orange, as orange also signifies and represents a variety of emotions, particularly wisdom.

Buddhists refer to the sacral chakra as the 'hara', which signifies the center of our most profound wisdom and expression. Activating the sacral chakra enables us to discover meaning, serenity, and happiness in life. Orange has a very sensual energy, and to maintain a balanced sacral chakra, it is necessary to incorporate this color into your life. Orange is also associated with the liver, bladder, and colon. These organs are responsible for the production and regulation of various hormones in the body, as well as the regulation of vital processes such as digestion.

In addition, they are governed by your sacral chakra. An underactive or overactive sacral chakra causes digestive issues, body aches, cramping, and hormonal imbalance. It can also result in aggression, anxiety, and the inability to express and control one's emotions.

In contrast, when the sacral chakra is in harmony, your senses feel alive. You appreciate physical and sensual sensations, have a robust metabolism and sexuality, and experience inner happiness and tranquility. In addition, a balanced sacral chakra facilitates self-expression and communication of sentiments and ideas with others.

Due to the calming and nurturing effects of orange, it is known to generate effects such as an increased sense of exhilaration and activity, appetite, socialization, increased mental activity, and contentment, as well as increase the brain's oxygen supply. It also facilitates the decision-making process by enhancing your self-assurance and understanding of situations and experiences.

This gorgeous hue of citrus fruits is also associated with a nutritious diet, vitamin C, and warmth and fire. This vibrant hue works marvels in attracting attention and making you noticeable enough for others to notice you. This is why it is also incorporated into brand insignia so that they are simple for the audience to remember.

Orange is frequently utilized in the branding, interior decoration, architecture, and furnishings of restaurants and hotels due to its ability to stimulate appetite and attract attention. For example, orange placemats and tablecloths are commonly used in restaurants.

While the color has many wonderful associations and meanings, too much of it can make you self-centered, proud, arrogant, aggressive, and dominant, as well as indifferent to the needs of those around you. In contrast, a lack of this color in one's existence leads to loneliness, low self-esteem, and a lack of motivation. This is why it is essential to maintain a healthy balance in your existence.

Now that you are well-versed in the various meanings of the color and how it affects various facets of your life, let's examine its diverse interpretations.

Numerous Definitions of Orange

It represents the Dutch Royal family in the Netherlands, whereas in Columbia it is a symbol of fecundity and sexuality. In many Eastern cultures, orange is a symbol of pleasure, good health, humility, love, and purity, as Buddhist monks often wear orange robes.

Interpreting Auras

Your aura is a field of energy and magnetism that surrounds you and every other living thing. It is also known as the HEF, or Human Energy Field. Your aura consists of seven interconnected layers that make up your energy body. The strata represent your emotional, physical, mental, astral, and divine characteristics.

Auras vary from person to person, and your aura contains information about your life. It can also affect your ability to communicate with others. The aura of most individuals has a 3-foot radius, extending between 18 inches and 2 feet from the body. People who have experienced tragedy and trauma have an aura that is larger than usual. It's not something most people can see, but if you develop your clairvoyant abilities, you'll be able to perceive it. It is also evident that they employ Kirlian photography.

Each color within the aura has a unique meaning. Additionally, clairvoyants can detect energy patterns and blockages. By merely observing the aura, they are able to discern numerous details. Before you can discern or perceive another person's aura, you must first be able to perceive your own energy field. When you strive to open your third eye, you will be able to perceive auras and more.

Self-Awareness

You must be self-aware to see auras and correctly interpret them. You must understand where your energy ends and another's begins in order to avoid taking on other people's characteristics as your own and projecting your traits onto others. Auras can be plainly interpreted by individuals like spirit mediums, remote viewers, etc. They are able to assess the body, detect imbalances, obstructions, personality defects and strengths, and even see past or future events in the subject's life.

Edgar Cayce once stated, "an aura is an effect, not a cause." The vibrations emitted by every atom and molecule tell a story about itself, its structure, and its purpose. The human eye interprets these vibrations as colors. As individuals' souls traverse the domains, they adjust and alter their patterns in response to the opportunities presented to them. Thus, at any given time, a soul will emit vibrations that tell the story of itself and its current state." So when I see a man's radiance, I see him as he truly is. I have learned through experience to discern a great deal from the intensity of hues. In other words, if you want to determine whether you and another person are likely to be on the same wavelength, you can tell instantaneously by observing their aura. You will be able to discern if a loved one is struggling, even if they appear to be fine, and offer them solace and support if they are willing to accept it.

With your eyes, you may not be able to detect people's auras immediately, but you've probably sensed them before. When someone enters a room and you sense the impulse to move away from them, it's because you've detected something negative about their aura. Similarly, there are individuals you simply enjoy being around. Because your aura and theirs blend harmoniously. Seeing auras elevates this sensation to a whole new level.

Recognizing Your Aura

Your aura is unique, but as it mingles with the auras of those around you, your interactions with them will impact your aura, and vice versa. It is not necessary to have a similar aura to another person in order to get along, but people with similar auras tend to get along better with one another than with others.

Now, let's discuss how to see your own aura.

As you stand in front of a mirror, ensure that the background is neutral or white so that no colors distort your view.

Ensure that you are donning white or gray clothing.

Maintain your focus on your forehead. Spend one minute focusing on it while ensuring your pupils are relaxed.

As you observe, a halo will begin to form around the contour of your cranium. It will initially appear as a soft, white radiance.

Continue to monitor your forehead, and you will observe a change over time.

Suppose you have been concentrating for some time. In this case, you will see afterimages of your aura, which will appear as a negative rendition of your aura's actual hue, so keep this in mind.

Utilize Your Imagination

When you become acquainted with your own energy, you can also detect auras using your intuition. How to determine your aura:

Relax and get comfortable. You may stand if you so choose.

Keep your hands approximately six inches from your head, in front of you. You should have your palms facing you.

Slowly lower your wrists and maintain a distance of six inches.

As you move your palms, sense your energy and intuitively determine the hues you believe you are emitting. You must believe what you receive.

If it helps, you can close your eyes to gain a correct sense of your energy and ground yourself.

Aura Colors and Their Significance

Auras reveal a great deal about your current mental state and past life experiences. To accurately interpret auras, you must understand what each color represents.

Blue indicates that you are observing a survivor. This individual has mastered the art of remaining tranquil and relaxed in times of difficulty or tension. It indicates that their nervous system is tranquil, that they live a balanced existence, and that they are able to transform agitated energies into peace.

The color turquoise indicates you are gazing at someone with a lot of vitality. This individual is a genuine influencer in the realist sense, and they possess a dynamic quality. They are organizers who can handle multiple tasks simultaneously. When they must concentrate on a single task, they become fatigued. They make outstanding managers.

The aura of a healer whose energy is restful and calming is green. These individuals are natural gardeners. The greater the verdant, the greater their serenity. It is the color of nature, and these individuals are easygoing and comforting, just as being in nature is.

The color purple represents spirituality. It does not reside permanently in the aura, but appears as a temporary haze or flame. This color also indicates that the individual possesses psychic abilities and is exceedingly wise, particularly in spiritual matters.

Red emanates a sense of materialism. This individual is preoccupied with their physique and other material possessions. Red is a color associated with the heart and circulation, as well as a dense color. It could also be a sign of vigor and fervor, making it either alluring or repulsive.

Pink is a combination of the highest and lowest frequency colors, purple and red. It is also transient, like purple, and will only occasionally appear. This indicates that the individual has achieved a balance between the spiritual and the material.

Yellow is a symbol of liberty and happiness. This aura indicates intelligence, inspiration, and enlightenment. Those with this aura are charitable and have an inner pleasure that cannot be shaken. It is also an indication that this person is highly spiritually developed, and if they are not already, they would make excellent spiritual teachers.

Gray, brown, and sulfur are negative colors that appear darker than the individual's background and appear as haze or radiance. The colors represent melancholy, negative thoughts, rage, illness, and even mortality. These colors indicate that the individual's mind and body are out of sync, a condition that only worsens as they near death.

Purifying Your Aura

What should you do if you detect obstructions, negative energies, and other life-disturbing issues in your aura? Just as you can neglect your health or personal maintenance, you can also neglect your aura. In the same way that neglecting your health can lead to problems in the future, ignoring your aura can cause problems, such as mood disorders such as anxiety and depression, etc.

Negative emotions that you haven't dealt with, negative thoughts that others have about you, unresolved past-life issues, and other day-to-day concerns can all contribute to problems with your aura. When you have a past-life reading, you will be able to determine the origin of some of your issues. Emotional and spiritual issues can also contaminate your aura, making it difficult to cleanse. When you are weighed down by energy blockages, you will feel disconnected, negative, and exhausted. If this is a persistent condition for you, it is time to purify your aura. This is how:

Relax and recline comfortably. Expect this process to take fifteen minutes, and please do not interrupt. Turn off all electronic devices and wear comfortable clothing.

Concentrate on your breathing. Breathe in and out without pausing between inhalations and exhalations.

Feel the air you inhale travel directly to your fingertips and digits as you breathe.

Observe a brilliant white light shining above your head.

This light will steadily envelop your entire body, leaving you feeling safe, adored, and toasty.

Observe this radiance emanating from you and filling the room. Imagine it touching everything in the room and extending outwards. All that the light touches is auspicious, holy, and secure.

This light represents affection and safety.

Imagine inhaling the light and exhaling a dark vapor that dissolves into the surrounding light. Continue until the light you exhale is pure white.

Permit yourself to exit this session slowly and tenderly.

Other Methods to Purge Your Aura

Get in shape. Begin consuming healthier and exercising more. Take in more fluids and soak up some sun. Get more slumber. If this requires you to organize your life more effectively, do so. Avoid processed foods and practice consuming methodically so you can recognize when you're satisfied and avoid overloading. Realize that these changes are not temporary, but rather represent long-term lifestyle adjustments. Therefore, before you commence, you must recognize that you deserve superior treatment. Knowing this will assist you in resisting the urge to return to old hazardous behaviors.

Put an end to negative notions. You cannot afford to dwell on negative thoughts for too long. Your aura will become very opaque and dark if you do so. Instead of focusing on the negative, make an effort to develop a positive disposition. This means planning for the occurrence of a poor disposition. Create an inventory of the things that make you feel good, those that cannot help but make you feel lighter and joyful. You know what you enjoy doing, whether it's spending time with family, exercising, playing a video game, meditating, taking a siesta, listening to amazing music, dancing, etc. If you have issues with feeling good, spend time with positive individuals who know how to pull you out of your negativity.

Utilize crystals to your benefit. Place them on your bed and window ledges. Crystals will protect you from negative energy and help you find inner calm.

Frequent Requested Information

How can I determine whether auras are genuine or imagined?

Yes, auras are genuine. Everyone and everything has a distinct energy signature. Auras are merely the energy's emanation. If it helps, you can consider a person's aura to be their personal energy if you can't yet see the hues. People possess an unmistakable "feel" about them. Such is their aura.

Exist individuals who do not possess auras?

No, not at all. As long as you are alive and a part of this world, you will undoubtedly have your own unique energy signature.

What are auras similar to?

If you utilize Kirlian photography, you will observe that the image resembles an egg-shaped circle encircling the body. The aura is depicted by artists as a luminous sphere or halo encompassing the body.

What methods can I use to better perceive my aura?

Suppose you do not have a camera designed to detect auras. In this case, you can simply perceive your energy field by blurring your vision and mildly narrowing your eyes while looking in the mirror. In addition, if you use your peripheral vision, you are more likely to see your aura. When you stare directly at your aura, you won't be able to see it, but if you turn away from it, you may be able to see the light or hues emanating from it. Recognize that it will take some time and effort.

Whose aura is simpler to perceive, mine or others'?

It depends on how proficiently you use your third sight. Additionally, when detecting your own aura, you can concentrate on yourself, meditate, and take the time to communicate with your own spiritual energy. You have no control over other people's auras, and they may not be in the room long enough for you to catch up on what they're giving off. Having said that, some individuals have auras that are difficult to ignore or overlook.

Why do I perceive a mixture of colors in an aura?

Our aura consists of distinct strata with their own hues. Some of these hues are more prominent than others, depending on who is observing and what they are experiencing or thinking. The more vibrant or energetic a person is, the more vivacious or vibrant the colors. The darker the colors, the greater the amount of negative emotions and energies they are experiencing. In addition, the fact that you are unable to perceive any colors is not cause for alarm.

What do each of the aura's layers represent?

The first stratum is the corporeal one, which is diminished by your daily activities and restored while you slumber. It relates to health, physical amenities, and the five senses. The next layer is the astral, which is your emotional layer and the source of self-love.

This is followed by the lower mental layer, in which the majority of your thoughts and reasoning reside. This is the layer that your waking self must employ every day. This stratum allows you to concentrate, study, work, and act in accordance with your values and beliefs. The next layer is the higher mental layer, which connects the other layers and enables you to care for others and yourself. Your spiritual layer allows you to connect with other people spiritually, and it continues to shine brighter when you share, teach, and connect with others on spiritual matters. Your intuitive layer is administered by your third eye. It's all about your ideal existence, your inclinations, and your intuition. Last but not least, there is the absolute layer, which is responsible for containing and balancing all other layers.

How can I tell if other people's auras are compatible with mine?

Work with the color meanings you've been given. Generally, good energy will always "vibe" well with good energy.

Negative and positive auras will just not mesh well together.

Now that you know how to read auras, let's talk about the psychic ability you can gain and use in your everyday life.

Throat Chakra

Truth is expressed through the Throat Chakra as it seeks harmony. The Chakra is the focal point of communication, expression, manifestation, and truth. As it is connected to the etheric realm of intuitive powers, an open Throat Chakra paves the way for psychic abilities and deeper intuition.

Learning about the Throat Chakra

The fifth main Chakra, the larynx Chakra, is located at the base of the larynx.

Vishuddha is the Sanskrit term for the Throat Chakra, which translates to "pure."

The color of the Throat Chakra is blue, and its center may contain purple tints. Depending on a person's disposition, emotional state, or physical health, the color of their eyes can vary from a brighter blue to a dimmer blue. The aura of the Throat Chakra may appear to be an indistinct shade of purple.

The Throat Chakra can be accessed via a Bija Mantra or a singular sound/vibration. The Throat Chakra syllable is "HAM" which is pronounced on the E note at a frequency of 672 Hz.

The Mudra, or hand gesture, for the Throat Chakra. Mudra is performed by resting the palms on the torso. With the palms facing upwards, interlace the fingers. The wrists must be situated on the thorax with the forearms pointing away from the torso and outwards. The two digits must be interlaced with their points contacting.

"I speak the truth with conviction, openly and freely" is an affirmation for the Throat Chakra.

Influence of the Throat Chakra on the Body and Soul

The Throat Chakra has an effect on:

Jaws

Mouth Neck

the thyroid gland of the throat

The energy center of the Throat Chakra is the pursuit of interior fulfillment in the pursuit of truth.

Characteristics of the Throat Chakra's Behavioral Patterns

The Throat Chakra is the starting point for psychic development. It is the Chakra that establishes a connection to the etheric realm and is the spiritual gateway to intuition.

The Throat Chakra is the communication Chakra that opens more than just the earthly communication channel. It opens the channels of communication to the spiritual domain and enables one to not only see but also sense the truth of everything around them. It is the Chakra that provides a person with amazing ideas, inspiration, and the ability to articulate their truth.

The Throat Chakra is related to the ability to perceive.

Friday is the day associated with the Throat Chakra. The element in question is ether.

The following gemstones are associated with the Throat Chakra:

Amazonite

Aquamarine

Lapis Lazuli

Turquoise

The Throat Chakra: Significance and Symbols

The symbol for the Throat Chakra is a flower with sixteen petals, typically a lotus flower. It is a deep blue color with white lines and paler hues of blue. In the center of the flower is either a crescent or two interconnected triangles, with a circle contained within the inverted triangle.

The color blue in the symbol represents trust, wisdom, faith, and purity.

The crescent represents the purity of the moon as spiritual purification.

As the Throat Chakra is located between the mind and the heart, it connects emotion to consciousness.

Advantages of a Clear Throat Chakra

When the Throat Chakra is open, an individual can readily communicate with others. People are naturally drawn to those with an open Throat Chakra because they come across as compassionate, approachable, and trustworthy.

As the first of the three higher spiritual Chakras, it is the conduit between the lower and higher Chakras. It is both the interpreter and the portal between the physical realm and the Divine illumination.

A person believes they can communicate on all levels and have a deeper comprehension of their surroundings. Not only is communication with other humans made possible, but also with the cosmos. You feel as though you comprehend nature itself.

Included among the benefits of an open Throat Chakra are:

Ability to communicate your needs and desires effectively.

Having more compassion as a result of a greater capacity to comprehend others.

Being able to analyze and freely articulate your emotions.

Unblocking the path to original thought.

Feeling increasingly intuitive.

Being able to differentiate between the truth and falsehoods.

What Can Obstruct the Throat Chakra?

Numerous factors can obstruct a person's Chakras. These occurrences occur in ordinary life without our awareness. You probably do not realize that they are causing various obstructions or tension to your body, mind, and spirit because you deal with them on a daily basis.

Among the causes of a Throat Chakra blockage are the following:

Depression

negative notions

A high-stress occupation that induces apprehension.

Associating with noisy and aggressive individuals.

Being compelled to leave your comfort zone.

Lies, animosity, and envy.

Symptoms of an Unbalanced or Blocked Throat Chakra

When the Throat Chakra is blocked or out of balance, a person loses the desire to communicate. They will feel as though the connection between their mouth and brain has been severed, as the words they wish to speak do not materialize.

Signs of an unbalanced or blocked Throat Chakra include:

You sense you have forgotten your purpose in life.

You are unable to realize your life's ambitions.

You cannot articulate your requirements, wishes, or desires.

You have a persistent sore larynx that may make you feel as though something is obstructing it.

You frequently experience hoarseness, a parched larynx, or laryngitis.

You suffer from chronic neck discomfort and mandible or neck tension.

Your thyroid is causing you difficulties.

You experience anxiety when contemplating public speaking or even speaking with others.

You have persistent dental issues.

You constantly suffer from migraines.

2 Heart Center

Opening the Heart Chakra has a profound effect on how a person expresses their emotions and makes them more receptive to love. It is the Chakra that is concerned with the exchange of emotions. When a person's heart is open, they are able to determine who is deserving of their affection and have increased emotional intelligence.

Knowledge of the Heart Chakra

The fourth main Chakra, located in the center of the thorax near the heart, is the Heart Chakra.

The Sanskrit term for the Heart Chakra is Anahata, which means unassailable or unstruck.

Green is the color of the Heart Chakra. Depending on a person's disposition or health, the green will become lighter, darker, or tinged with subtle yellow hues. The aura color of the Heart Chakra is either faint or indistinct pink.

"YAM" is the Bija Mantra (sound or vibration) for the Heart Chakra, and it operates at three distinct frequencies and notes:

Upper Heart Chakra — The frequency is 624 Hz and the note is D.#

Middle section of the Heart Chakra — The frequency is 594 Hz and the note is D.

Listen to the lower section of the Chakra — the frequency is 552 Hz and the note is C#.

The Heart Chakra Mudra: Place the left hand on the left thigh and the right hand on the chest. Each hand's fingertips should be extended flat against the body. Create an O shape by connecting the index finger and forefinger ends of each hand.

The love that fills my heart, allows me to recuperate, and provides me with fortitude.

The Heart Chakra Affects the Physical Body and Soul

The Heart Chakra is the emotional energy core. It connects the three lower Chakras to the three higher Chakras.

The Heart Chakra affects the Arms

Hands

Heart Lungs

Thymus duct

The Heart Chakra is the source of energy for:

Emotions

Trust Forgiveness

Compassion

Behavioral Traits of the Heart Chakra

As they are located in the center of the thorax, the heart and lungs are the organs most affected by the Heart Chakra.

The Heart Chakra is the intermediate Chakra, where the lower Chakras merge with the higher Chakras. This is viewed as a transition from the material to the divine.

Touch is the perception that is affiliated with the Heart Chakra.

The day of the week associated with the Heart Chakra is Thursday. Air is the related element.

The following stones are associated with the Heart Chakra:

Clear quartz

Emerald

Green Calcite

Jade

Pink/Rose Quartz

The Heart Chakra Symbol and Its Signification

The Heart Chakra is represented by a flower with twelve petals (typically a lotus flower) encircling a circle. Within the flower's circle are two intersecting triangles that form a six-pointed star.

The symbol represents:

Acceptance

Compassion Empathy

Emotion

Forgiveness

Passion Trust

Green and white are the colors of the Heart Chakra symbol, which signify:

Peace

Harmony

Union

Benefits of a Heart Chakra that is Open

When the Heart Chakra is open, an individual no longer feels emotionally closed off or isolated.

The energy of the Heart Chakra travels through the centers that enable a person to recognize that their ego is holding them back. A deeper comprehension of one's emotional core demonstrates that it is acceptable to love and be loved. But true love cannot exist when the ego stands in the way.

Among the advantages of having an open Heart Chakra are:

Loving oneself

embracing affection

The capacity to adore

a deeper comprehension of human emotion

Feeling profound empathy

exhibiting more sympathy

Influences that Can Obstruct the Heart Chakra

Emotions render a person delicate, open, and susceptible. Humans are more reclusive than ever in a world that is so exposed. They conceal themselves behind their personalities and facades, allowing the world to perceive only their outward appearance. By concealing and closing down, we block the Heart Chakra's energy flow.

Among the factors that can lead to a blocked Heart Chakra are:

Being conceited

morally dependent

Being overly reliant on another

Sensing abandonment or rejection
Sensing envy, rage, or resentment

Oversharing

Not communicating your feelings

Turning away from emotions

Falsely claiming to be something one is not

Heart Chakra Imbalance or Blockage Indicators

When the Heart Chakra is unbalanced or obstructed, there are two possible outcomes. Either they become emotionally dependent on the other person, or they develop jealousy and suspicion. They may emotionally withdraw or become capricious, provocative, or insulting. They may turn their backs completely on emotions.

Among the indications of a Heart Chakra imbalance or blockage are:

Causing others sorrow by inability to devote

Being neglectful

Having outbursts of rage

Behaving in a possessive or obsessive manner

Having social awkwardness

Being bashful

Having a reclusive or lone wolf personality

Easily becoming emotionally exhausted

feeling vindictive

Being excessively analytical

Being offensive

Chakra Stones

Chakra stones are various varieties of stones of various hues that are utilized to support chakra restoration.

Each chakra in the human organism has a specific color. If these chakras are not operating properly, their colors will change.

The purpose of chakra stones is to assist your chakras in achieving balance and a greater sense of calm and harmony. Chakra can become misaligned, as they are frequently compared to rotating energy wheels. Additionally, they can collapse into a lethargic turn or spin too quickly.

Because each chakra corresponds to a particular spiritual, emotional, physical, or mental aspect of our being, it is often felt when one of them loses its equilibrium.

As you learn more about how to use chakra stones to cope with such a scenario, you will find chakra stones to be useful in enabling you to anticipate such a situation. As previously taught, each chakra has its own color representation. Each chakra has its own symptoms of problems, and it is essential to observe attentively which problem or ailment reoccurs. Upon gaining a clear understanding of which chakra has a problem, it is essential to select the appropriate chakra stone to restore, cleanse, and balance that chakra.

Chakra stones can be chosen from a wide variety of crystals, as the ultimate aim is to find the optimal balance for optimal chakra function. If you accumulate and store precious stones for any other reason besides their restorative properties, you may be surprised to discover that you have items that are a solution to one or more of your chakras' issues.

Chakra stones are identical and serve the same function, regardless of whether one is more expensive, rare, or inherently attractive than the others. If you have the proper color, you can properly align your chakras.

Stone of Chakra for Root

Red and black stones are the correct stones to help you align your root chakra. You will feel more rooted, stable, and confident in yourself.

Ruby, Black Obsidian, Hematite, Smoky Quartz, Red Jasper, Jet, Black Onyx, Fire Opal, Bloodstone, and Red Garnet are the recommended stones for the root chakra.

You must position any of the aforementioned stones near to your pelvis and between your thighs for your root chakra. Consider the color crimson or black when contemplating a more robust core, a stronger passion for all things, and a happier, more stable foundation.

Stone for the Sacral Chakra

When your Sacral Chakra is overactive, you will experience frequent frustrations, and when it is underactive, you will lack happiness.

Numerous chakra stones, including Orange Calcite, Orange Aventurine,

Tiger's Eye, Orange Jasper, Carnelian, Sunstone, Fire Opal, Tangerine Quartz, and Brown Citrine, can help you align your sacral chakra.

When your Sacral Chakra is aligned, you will be inspired, motivated, and filled with the required enthusiasm.

Stone for the Solar Plexus Chakra

When your Solar Plexus Chakra is in alignment, you will have innovative and creative ideas. Yellow gemstones, such as Yellow Jasper, Amber, Golden Calcite, Rutilated Quartz, Moonstone, Citrine, Fire Opal, Pyrite, and Topaz, are the appropriate Chakra Stones to use to heal your Solar Plexus.

By aligning your Solar Plexus Chakra, you will feel goal-oriented, inspired, and self-assured. To use these stones on your Solar Plexus Chakra, lie face up and lay the stones 2 inches apart from your abdominal button. Consider the hue yellow and an extremely brilliant sunny day.

Stones for the Heart Chakra

When your chakras are aligned, you are more receptive and relaxed, ready to accept new relationships, maintain healthy ones, forgive, and experience love.

Green Aventurine, Emerald, Peridot, Rhodonite, Green Tourmaline, Rose Quartz, Green Moss Agate, Pink Tourmaline, Jade, Ruby, Chrysoprase, Malachite, Rhodochrosite, and Watermelon Tourmaline are recommended Chakra stones for aligning the heart chakra.

You will regain your optimism, fortify your relationships, and radiate affection.

Stones for the Throat Chakra

When your Throat Chakra is out of balance, you will have trouble expressing your thoughts, resulting in miscommunication and frustration.

Blue chakra stones will assist you in balancing your Throat Chakra. They include Blue aragonite, Lapis Lazuli, Angelite, Blue Apatite, Blue Calcite, Turquoise, Aquamarine, Sodalite, Blue Sapphire, and Blue Lace Agate.

When your larynx chakra is balanced, communication and self-expression become effortless.

Stones for the Third Eye Chakra

When the Third Eye is misaligned, you will be resistant to new ideas, unable to trust others, and your intuition will be off.

You will utilize Amethyst, Fluorite, Azurite, Blue Aventurine, Lapis Lazuli, Lolite, Celestite, Angelite, and Sugilite to stabilize your Third Eye Chakra.

When your Third Eye is aligned, your intuition will be stronger, your intellect will be clearer, and your problem-solving skills will be enhanced.

Chakra Stones for the Third Eye

If your Crown Chakra is unstable, you will feel anxious and be unable to think clearly. You will feel disoriented, and the majority or all of your existence will appear uncertain. You will feel as though you lack direction and purpose in life.

White Topaz, Moonstone, Blue Opal, Amethyst, Selenite, Blue Sapphire, White Calcite, and Clear Quartz are extremely beneficial chakra stones.

To heal your Crown Chakras, merely place the stones on the crown of your head and visualize violet or white light.

Your existence will be filled with illumination and meaning. You will also have a positive outlook on potential setbacks, and you will be able to work towards accomplishing your life objectives.

How to Know You Are Activating Your Chakras

Every thought, emotion, and experience we have pertains to our energy system and chakras. Because we use chakras constantly, it is crucial that we pay close attention to all aspects of our lives in order to determine when we are activating our chakras as well as when they are unbalanced or blocked. For instance, if I have controlling tendencies but am also highly energetic and motivated, it indicates that my chakras are out of balance and I must work to stabilize them. Below is a concise summary to assist you in comprehending the behavior of each chakra when it is open:

Understanding Open First Chakra-Root

You will have a robust constitution, a sense of fundamental safety and security, and a sense of being grounded. Your feet, bones, weight, adrenal glands, colon, and elimination will be healthy. The functionality of your practical existence will be outstanding.

Understanding the Activated Second Chakra-Sacral

You will have a balanced sexuality, positive life energy, an openness to change, and sound reproductive and urinary systems. You will also experience delight, and your second chakra will be neither overactive nor underactive.

Understanding Third Chakra-Solar Plexus in the Open

When your third chakra is activated, you will be able to accomplish your physical objectives. You will feel worthy of respect. There will be robust immune, digestive, muscular, and adrenal systems. There will be no significant allergic reactions.

Understanding the Heart's Fourth Chakra

When this chakra is open, you'll have compassion for others. In addition, you will be able to maintain healthy relationships, experience emotional fulfillment, feel connected to nature, and forgive others. You will demonstrate yourself and others compassion. Your lungs, wrists, limbs, thymus, and heart will be healthy.

Understanding the Fifth Chakra-Throat when It Is Open

You will have the ability to express yourself and your own truth when this chakra is activated. You will be able to listen, express yourself creatively, and have a healthy voice, jaw, ears, neck, shoulders, sinuses, and nostrils.

Understanding the Third Eye-Open Sixth Chakra

You will have a balanced intellect with other intelligence traits such as good concentration, perception, an outstanding memory, intuition, and the ability to see the "big picture." Your eyes, vision, hypothalamus, and pituitary gland will be healthy.

Understanding the Crown Seventh Chakra

If your seventh chakra is open, you will experience a sense of connection to a greater purpose and power; you will feel wiser, have inner serenity, a more developed consciousness, an acceptance of others, and a stable mind. You will have a pineal gland and cerebral cortex in good health.

How to Activate the Root Chakra (Red)

One of the most effective methods to activate your chakra is to first become grounded, that is, to attach yourself to the earth. To accomplish this, keep your feet shoulder-width apart and shift your pelvis forward while bending your knees slightly. Distribute your eight evenly by maintaining a balanced body. After grounding yourself, sit cross-legged and gently affix your index finger to your sternum.

Visualize the root chakra as a crimson flower whose petals are filled with energy and which opens to reveal four petals that are filled with energy. Twenty to thirty minutes of contracting, holding, and releasing perineum respiration. This should assist you in balancing your root chakra.

How to Open the Sacra

To open your second chakra, begin by sitting on your knees with your back erect or in an upright position. Rest your hands in your lap with the palms' inner sides facing upwards. Touch the rear digits of your right hand with your left hand, so that your left hand is under your right hand. Connect the knuckles of both palms. Concentrate on the chakra and the area below the navel that it represents. While gently breathing, recite the word "VAM" in silence. Perform this activity for at least 30 minutes, or until you feel thoroughly relaxed. This exercise will cleanse your mind and open your sacral chakra.

Opening the Solar Plexus Chakra

Maintain an erect stance on your knees. Place your hand just below the upper abdomen, in front of the stomach, where the solar plexus chakra is located. Put your fingers together with your thumps closed and point them in the opposite direction. Concentrate on your chakra and its location. Clearly chant the word "RAM" while continuing to contemplate chakra and its meaning, as well as its impact on various aspects of life. Repeat this procedure until you feel calm and tidy.

How to Activate the Heart Chakra

Cross your legs while sitting down. Attach the index digits of both palms to the thumbs. Place the right hand below the breastbone and the left hand on the left knee. Maintain this position for at least twenty minutes while contemplating your heart chakra and its location in the center of your chest. Silently chant the word "YAM" as you continue to unwind and focus on your heart chakra. Continue the practice until you no longer feel dirty. After a few moments of practicing this technique and opening your heart chakra, you will experience a deep sense of compassion.

How to Activate the Throat Chakra

Again, begin by kneeling on the ground. Cross each finger's interior and remove the thumps. Attach the tops of your thumps together. Concentrate on your throat chakra and what it represents, which is located at the base of your larynx. While continuing to contemplate your throat chakra and how it affects your life, recite the word "HAM" in a quiet but distinct manner. Ten to fifteen minutes of this will induce feelings of relaxation and hygiene.

How to Activate the Third Eye Chakra

Sit with your legs crossed. Place your palms beneath your chest. While brushing their crowns with your middle finger, you should point it away from you and extend it away from you. Concentrate on the third eye chakra and the part of the eyes that it represents. Chant silently the word "AUM" or "OM." Allow your body to naturally unwind as you continue to contemplate your chakra and its impact on your life. Practice for at least 20 minutes until you feel clean and/or focused enough to generate brilliant ideas to achieve your objectives.

How to Activate the Crown Chakra

Cross your legs while seated. Cross your fingers with the exception of your ring and pinky fingers, which should touch at the top and point away from you and upwards. The right thumb should be positioned above the left thumb. Concentrate on the crown chakra, which represents the summit of your cranium.

www.ingramcontent.com/pod-product-compliance
Lightning Source LLC
Chambersburg PA
CBHW050239120526
44590CB00016B/2151